24 Folds to Pocket Perfection

The Pocket Square Guide for Every Man

ALEXIS BURKE

Preface

Thank you for taking the time to read "24 Folds to Pocket Perfection: The Pocket Square Guide for Every Man." The pocket square is a subtle yet effective accent that, regardless of fashion, signifies refinement in men's dress. This book is an exploration into the science and art of folding, styling, and becoming an experienced pocket square user, a journey that goes into the nuances of personal expression as well as the fabric and stitching.

The pocket square is a popular fashion accessory that may be found on the breast pockets of both celebrities and everyday men. The goal of this book is to explain the beauty hidden inside those folds. From the history that pervades every minute crease to the rigorous consideration of fabric, size, and location, we set out on a journey to find the potential of this seemingly insignificant accessory.

Not just folds, the twenty-four folds presented in these pages are chapters in the story of smart clothing. Every fold has a distinct personality that is appropriate for a variety of occasions and fashion preferences. Beyond the folds, we travel through a landscape of harmonized colours, well chosen materials, and the skillful dance of suit and tie accessorizing.

This book is more than simply a how-to guide; it's an invitation to boost your style, add a touch of classic elegance to your wardrobe, and discover that the pocket square is more than just an accessory; it's a sign of your own particular style narrative. So, may your journey through "24 Folds to Pocket Perfection" be filled with creativity, inspiration, and the joy of discovering beauty one fold at a time.

Table of Content

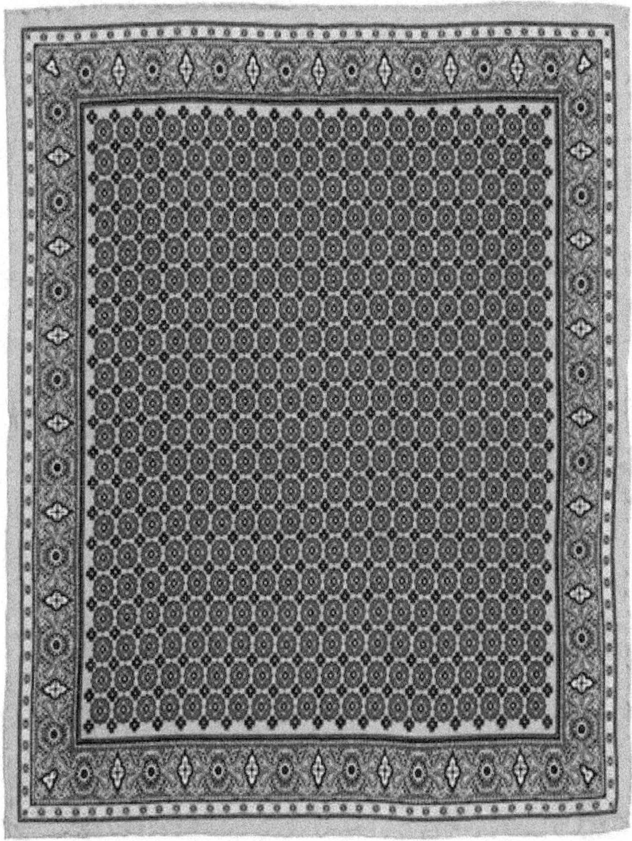

A POCKET SQUARE

Chapter 1

Introduction

A pocket square is a little piece of fabric that is used to cover the front of a jacket or shirt. It is meant to complete the look and is usually worn in the breast pocket. Although any fabric can be used to produce a pocket square, cotton or silk are the most popular. A pocket square is typically three inches by three inches.

A pocket square is a small piece of fabric that fits into the breast pocket of a man's jacket. It is typically made from silk, cotton, or linen. Originally, it was used as a decoration to show off the gentleman's wealth and status, as well as to protect his handkerchief.

Pocket squares are now worn with a variety of garment pieces, including blazers, jackets, and suits.

Rather than being an ornament given out at weddings or used as décor, the pocket square is now employed to add some flair to your wardrobe while out on the town.

Brief History of Pocket Square

Some believe that the pocket square originated in ancient Egypt, when little linen cloths were dyed red to represent their use as decorative goods and emblems of wealth. However, this is a significant leap of faith because little scraps of coloured cloth don't typically convert into what we call a pocket square in this day and age.

Some credit it to the Romans, who used fabric to start the Gladiatorial Games, with the Emperor dropping his handkerchief to signify the start of the competition, or the Ancient Greeks, who always carried a cloth scented with perfume to ensure they had a pleasant smell nearby.

Some claim that Catholics have worn white handkerchiefs on their left arms as a symbol of their devotion to God and the church since the 800s, when the handkerchief was first used as an ornament.

Finally, a commonly acknowledged hypothesis states that King Richard II of England was the first to adorn his throne with a handkerchief as a fashion accessory between 1377 and 1399. As a result, while it is clear that people have been using material squares for hundreds, if not thousands, of years, we believe that many of these romantic explanations fail to make a clear connection between what is true of the modern pocket square and its 600-year history.

Becoming a Fashion Accessory

Beginning in the 1400s, the upper classes in Europe began to use handkerchiefs as more useful tools or as fashionable accessories. By now, as yet another symbol of wealth and prestige, pocket squares and pocket handkerchiefs were constructed from more exotic fabrics, such as silk, and embroidered in exquisite patterns. They continued to exist in a variety of forms and sizes up until this point, and just like the Greeks, the French nobility scented their handkerchiefs to mask the smells of the era brought on by a widespread lack of bathing facilities.

It is believed that Catherine de Medici of Florence brought the finest lace and needlework patterns from Italy to France during the 16th century. These handkerchiefs were handed down from generation to generation and were thought to be very valuable. The style and quality of the lace being used frequently created the worth. The Tudor Monarchs carried on this particular tradition, giving handkerchiefs as New Year's presents to both Queen Mary and Queen Elizabeth. From that point on, giving handkerchiefs to royalty became commonplace.

According to a well-known legend, Marie Antoinette convinced her husband, King Louis XVI, that all fabric should have a standard size of 16" by 16" because she saw it was improper to have handkerchiefs in a variety of sizes. This may help to explain why modern objects typically have certain shapes and sizes.

Chapter 2

The Twenty-four folds to Pocket Perfection.

We will examine Twenty-four (24) techniques for folding a pocket square in this section. This approach consists of the following:

1. The 3 Peaks fold
2. The 4 Stairs fold
3. The Slope fold
4. The Double winged puff fold
5. The Wave fold
6. The Cagney fold
7. The Fleur-de-Lis fold
8. The Ice cream Mountain fold
9. The Layer cake fold

10. The Bouquet fold

11. The Inverted triangle fold

12. The 3 Petals fold

13. The Scallop fold

14. The Spiral Staircase fold

15. The Monarch fold

16. The Summit fold

17. The Rabbit fold

18. The 3 Point Crown fold

19. The 4 angled Peaks fold

20. The Switchback fold.

21. The Fancy Diamond fold

22. The Wedge fold

23. The Tri-Fold Pocket Square Fold

24. The Christmas Tree Pocket Square Fold.

Now let's delve into each and every one of these folds.

1. The 3 Peaks fold

This fold is sharp and elegant just like you. Use solid color squares or ones with subtle prints for the best look. The steps involved includes the following:

1. Lay out a pocket square on a flat surface.

2. Fold diagonally to make a triangle.

3. Fold a second time to form a smaller triangle with overlapping corners.

4. Fold yet again ensuring the third corner overlaps the first two.

5. Fold the bottom corner back to create the proper width for your pocket.

6. Now fold the bottom corner up to make a base.

7. Tuck into your jacket and adjust if needed.

Below is a diagrammatic explanation of the 3 Peaks Fold:

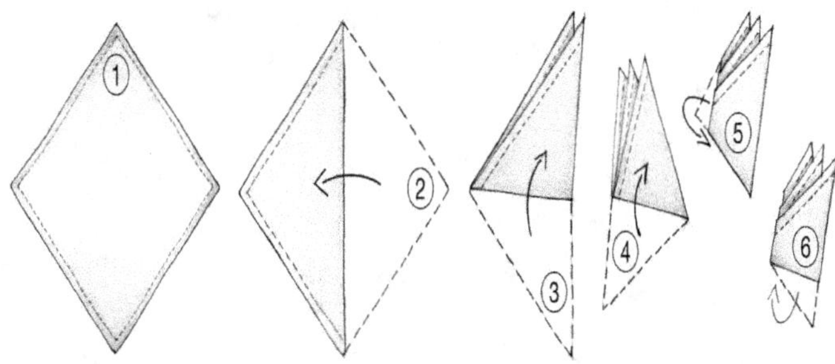

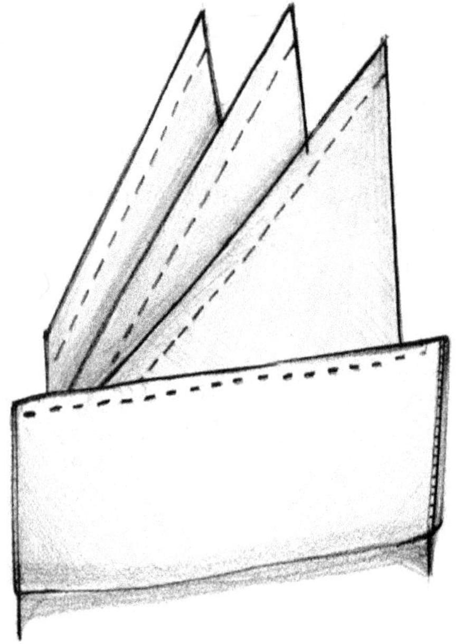

The 3 Peaks Fold

2. The 4 Stairs fold

This neat fold involves, not one, but two pocket squares! Because you're using two, you'll want to use smaller versions made with lightweight fabric so you don't add too much bulk to your pocket. It's best to combine two solid color pocket squares, or one solid along with one print. The steps involved includes the following:

1. Lay both of your pocket squares flat and smooth out.

2. Fold both pocket squares in half diagonally to create two triangles.

3. Lay one pocket square over the other so that one corner of the upper pocket square touches the center of the lower pocket square.

4. Fold the lower pocket square over the top of the upper pocket square.

5. Fold in the corner of the other pocket square at an angle so the other pocket square is still visible.

6. Now fold the other side over at an angle so that the lower pocket square is still visible.

7. Again, fold in the other side so the lower pocket square is visible.

8. Turn the pocket squares so the stairs are facing to the right.

9. Fold the bottom under to form the base.

10. Carefully place it in your jacket pocket and tidy up if needed.

Below is a diagrammatic explanation of the 4 Stairs Fold:

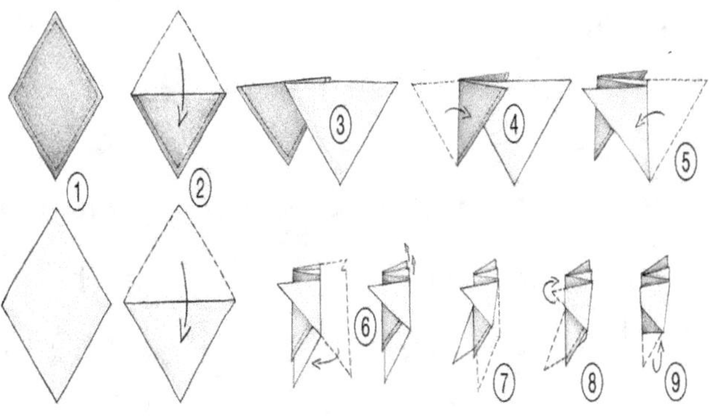

The 4 Stairs Fold

3. The Slope fold

This fold is versatile because it works just as well at the office as it does at a wedding. Use a subtle print for business and a solid color for pleasure. Any fabric will do, but a stiffer one works best to maintain the peaks. The steps involved includes:

1. Fold in half diagonally, allowing the corners to overlap.
2. Fold the bottom right corner up to form a sharp peak.
3. Fold the tip of the peak back.
4. Fold the left side over the front.
5. Fold the bottom right point back.
6. Slide it into your pocket and primp if needed.

Below is a diagrammatic explanation of the Slope Fold:

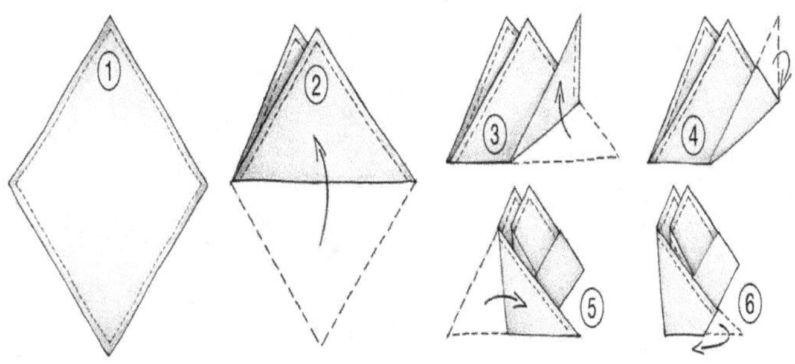

The Slope fold

4. The Double winged puff fold

For this fold, you'll need two pocket squares that are the same size. It's best to use a solid color along with a print. The steps involved includes:

1. Lay out both squares and smooth.
2. Fold both in half diagonally to form two triangles.
3. Select the pocket square that you want to be in the center and fold both tips of the triangle down to form a square.
4. Place the square down on top of the triangle approximately 1" higher than the lower triangle.
5. Fold down both corners of the triangle to wrap the square.

6. Fold the right and left corner of the square containing both pieces of fabric back so it will fit in your pocket.

7. Fold the bottom under to make a base.

8. Tuck the completed fold into your jacket and neaten if needed.

Below is a diagrammatic explanation of the double winged puff Fold:

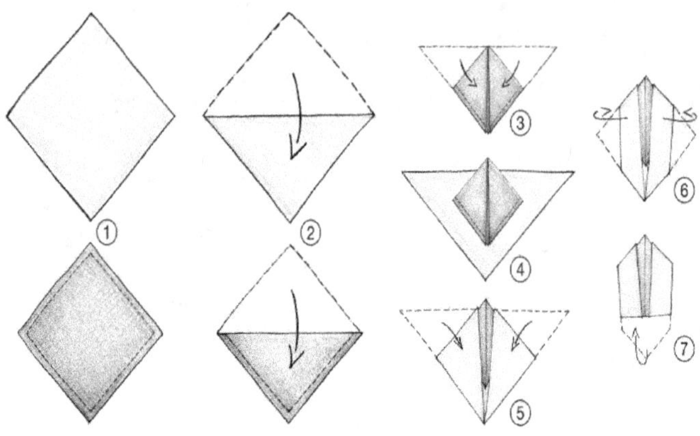

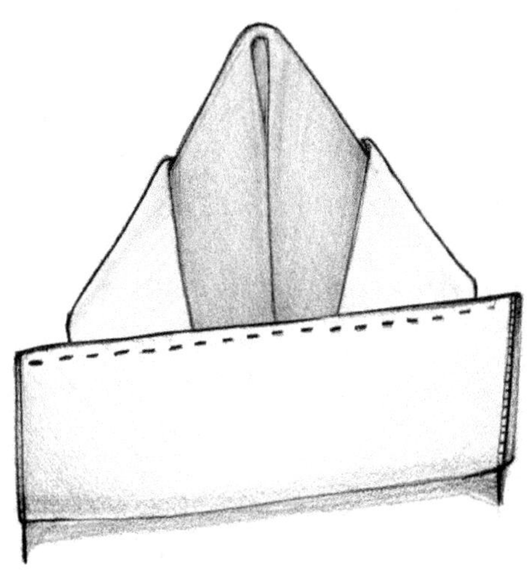

The Double Winged Puff fold

5. The Wave fold

Catch a wave with this neat fold. Looks great in solid color or patterned fabric. Its asymmetrical design draws the eye and keeps you looking sharp. The steps involved includes:

1. Flatten your pocket square on a smooth surface.
2. Next, fold one corner down to form a triangle.
3. Then, fold one side in so that it stops just below the other side.
4. Fold it in again so three corners are showing.
5. Fold so that the left side tip now touches the bottom tip.

6. Flip the pocket square over and ensure the tip if facing towards you.

7. Fold the side that's showing the corners down and create the 'wave'.

8. Neatly place the folded pocket square into your jacket pocket.

Below is a diagrammatic explanation of the wave Fold:

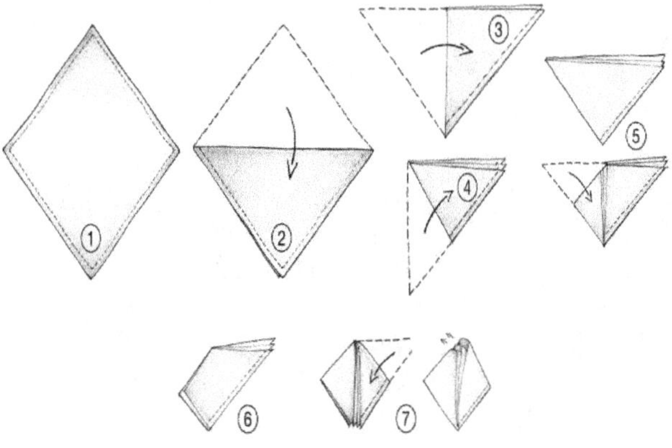

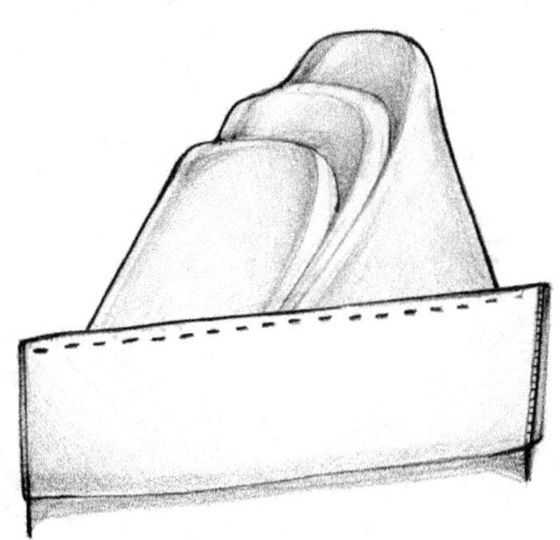

The Wave fold

6. The Cagney fold

This fold is fresh and fun with a floral look. It looks fabulous with solid color or printed pocket square, so the sky's the limit. The steps involved includes:

1. Smooth out the square on a flat surface.
2. Fold it in half diagonally to create a triangle.
3. Fold in one corner to form a second tip at the top.
4. Do the same on the other side to make the third tip at the top.
5. Fold in the right side again to decrease the size of the folded pocket square.

6. Next, do the same thing with the opposite side.

7. Fold up the bottom corner to make the center tip.

8. Gently place it in your jacket pocket and perfect the form.

Below is a diagrammatic explanation of the Cagney Fold:

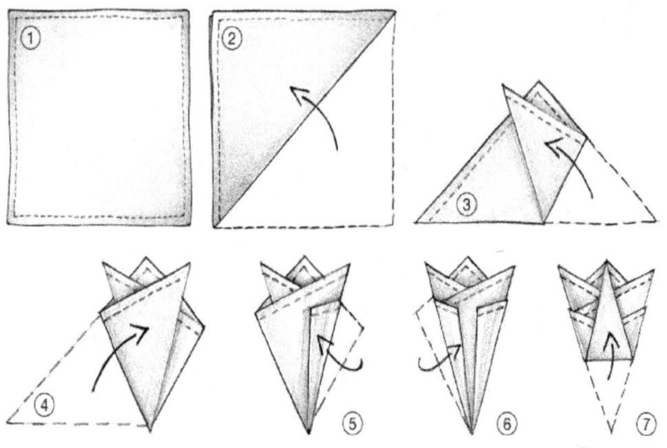

The Cagney fold

7. The Fleur-de-Lis fold

The iconic fleur-de-lis fold is a sleek way to showcase your favorite pocket square. Looks great in solid color pocket squares as well as bold printed ones. This fold works best with casual ensembles. The steps involved includes:

1. Lay out a pocket square and smooth flat.
2. Fold it in half diagonally to form a triangle.
3. Fold one corner up slightly above the base of the triangle.
4. Flip the pocket square over and fold the other corner up so it sits below the first corner.
5. Create three pleats on one side.

6. Repeat step 5 on the opposite side.

7. Next, fold the pocket square in half at the center point.

8. Secure the base of the pocket square with a rubber band.

9. Gently spread the tips of the 'flower' apart.

10. Lastly, tuck your creation in your pocket and arrange as needed.

Below is a diagrammatic explanation of the Fleur-de-Lis Fold:

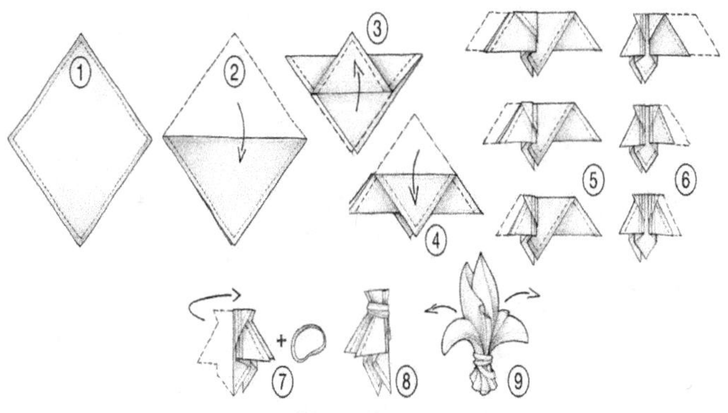

The Fleur-de-Lis fold

8. The Ice cream Mountain fold

I scream, you scream, we all scream for the ice scream mountain fold. This fun and whimsical fold is perfect for your bright solid color pocket squares. It requires two squares, so go crazy pairing up the fabrics. The steps involved includes:

1. Lay both pocket squares flat and smooth them out.
2. Fold both pocket squares in half diagonally to create two separate triangles.
3. Place one triangle over the other ensuring the bottom pocket square is visible along the long side.

4. Wrap the top pocket square with the bottom one ensuring the top of each square is showing.

5. Repeat step 4 with the other pocket square.

6. Next, fold in the bottom pocket square.

7. And then again with the other pocket square.

8. Fold the entire design in half along the center.

9. Fold back the left corner and refine the style.

10. Tuck it into your jacket pocket and enjoy!

Below is a diagrammatic explanation of the Ice cream Mountain Fold:

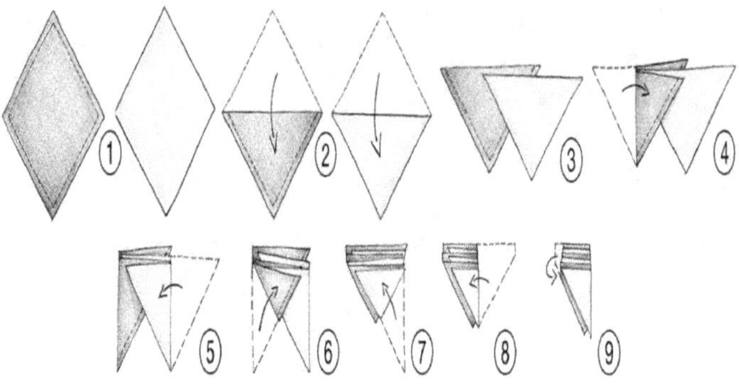

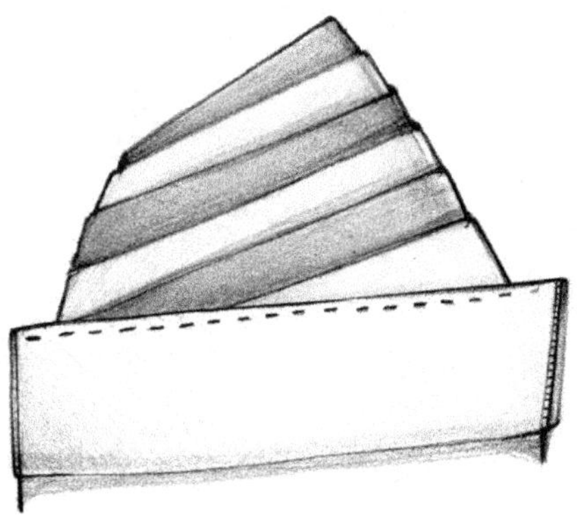

The Ice cream Mountain fold

9. The Layer cake fold

This delicious fold requires two pocket squares. Make sure you use smaller squares made of lightweight fabric so you don't add too much bulk to your pocket. This technique works best with two coordinating solid color pocket squares or one solid square paired with one printed one. The steps involved includes:

1. Lay both pocket squares flat on a flat, level surface.
2. Fold both pocket squares in half to form two rectangles.
3. Lay one pocket square over the other. The lower pocket square should be visible at the top to create the first 'layer'.

4. Next, make another layer by folding the other side over at a slight angle.

5. Form the final layer by folding the opposite side over again at an angle.

6. Adjust the width of the fold if necessary by folding back each side.

7. Tuck it into your jacket pocket and refine the look if needed.

Below is a diagrammatic explanation of the Layer Cake Fold:

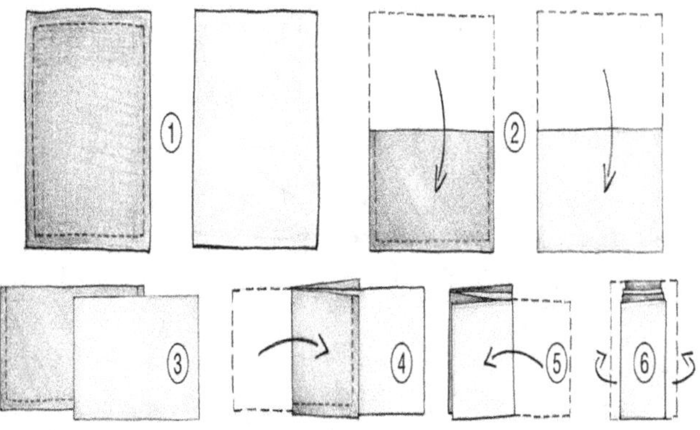

The Layer cake fold

10. The Bouquet fold

This dapper accordion fold looks like a bouquet of spring flowers sprouting from your pocket. Go wild and use bright colors and bold prints to add to the joyful nature of this look. A starched cotton pocket square is the best option for this fold. The steps involved includes:

1. Smooth out a square of fabric.
2. Pleat the fabric in eighths.
3. Fold the fabric using the accordion technique.
4. Fold the long rectangle in half.
5. Pinch the top together about 2" down.
6. Gently tuck the fold into your pocket and fluff if needed.

Below is a diagrammatic explanation of the Bouquet Fold:

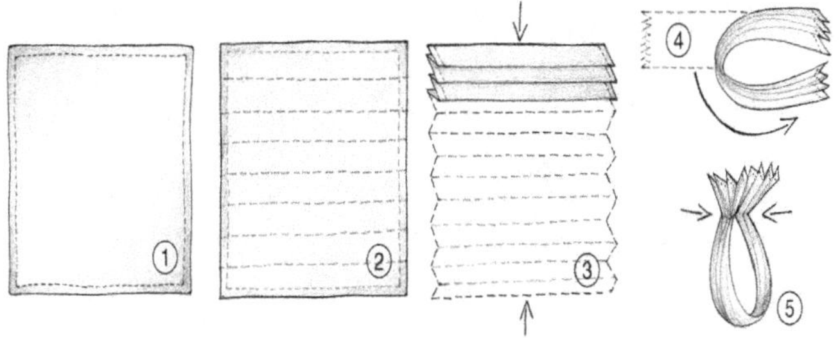

The Bouquet fold

11. The Inverted triangle fold

This fold is the perfect accent for both casual and formal ensembles. While subtle, it adds a touch of dapper elegance and keeps you looking chic all day. This fold is perfect for printed pocket squares. The steps involved includes:

1. Lay the square down flat.
2. Fold diagonally to create an even triangle.
3. Next, fold one side over to create a smaller triangle.
4. Fold it over yet again.
5. You may need to fold it over again if you're using a larger pocket square.

6. Rotate the pocket square so the long edge faces up.

7. Gently slide it into your pocket and adjust if needed. Cheers!

Below is a diagrammatic explanation of the Inverted triangle Fold:

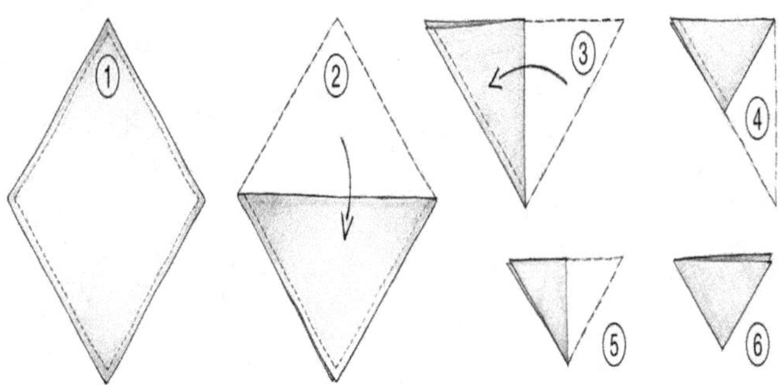

The Inverted triangle fold

12. The 3 Petals fold

This is simply a sleek, striking fold. Use a stiffer fabric in a solid color or one with an interesting print. The steps involved includes:

1. Start by smoothing your pocket square out.
2. Fold in half diagonally to make a triangle.
3. Fold up slightly one part of the triangle. Repeat on the other side.
4. Fold up the bottom corner to create the third 'petal'.
5. Carefully place the folded material in your pocket and perk the petals up.

Below is a diagrammatic explanation of the Inverted triangle Fold:

The 3 Petals fold

13. The Scallop fold

Bust out your origami skills to create this amazing elaborate fold. Use a solid color or printed pocket square depending on your mood. The steps involved includes:

1. Lay the pocket square flat and smooth it out.
2. Fold in half diagonally to make a triangle.
3. Fold in half again to make a smaller triangle.
4. Fold the right corner in.
5. Fold the left corner in.
6. Tuck it carefully into your pocket and step out in style.

Below is a diagrammatic explanation of the
Scallop Fold:

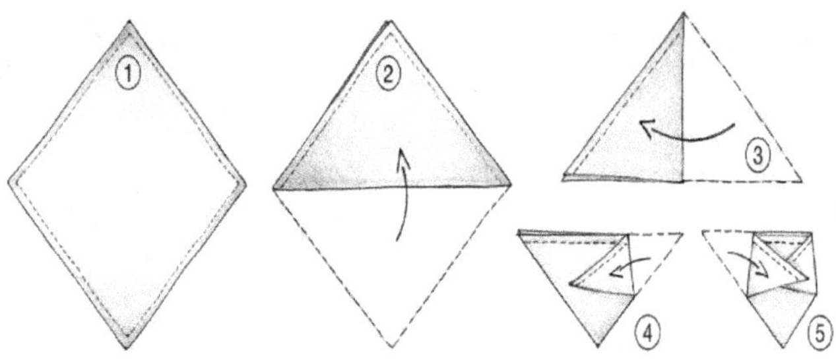

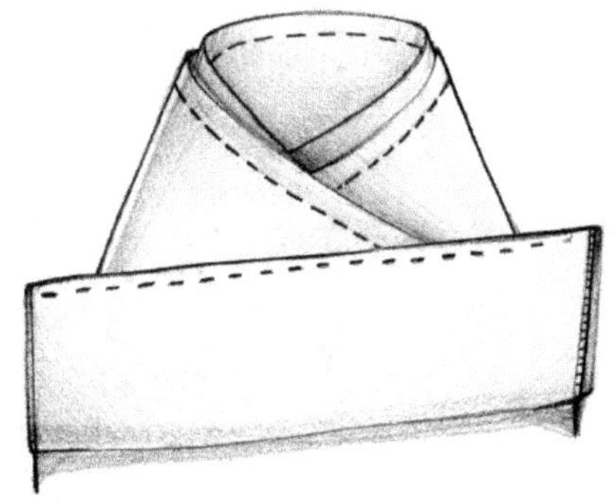

The Scallop fold

14. The Spiral Staircase fold

This intricate fold is perfect for the dapper gentleman. It's anything but plain and you'll stand out in the crowd while sporting it. This one works best with lightweight fabrics such as silk. The steps involved includes:

1. Lay down the pocket square and smooth it out.
2. Fold in half diagonally to create a triangle.
3. Fold one triangle down approximately 1" below the edge.
4. Fold it back down to create a pleat and flip it over.
5. Repeat steps 3 and 4 to create additional pleats.

6. Next, lay your pocket square down flat and fold it in half.

7. Create the 'spiral staircase' by rolling one side down and to the left to create the desired effect.

8. Finally, tuck it gently into your jacket pocket.

Below is a diagrammatic explanation of the Spiral Staircase Fold:

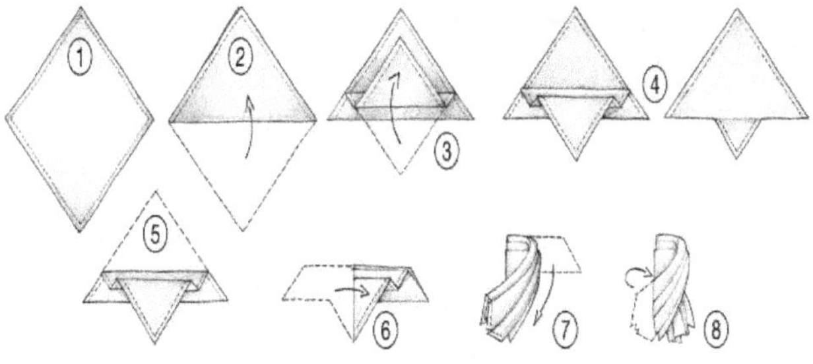

The Spiral Staircase fold

15. The Monarch fold

This is a clean and elaborate fold that's great for any pocket square color and print. To prevent too much bulk, it's best to use silk or other lightweight fabrics. The steps involved includes:

1. Smooth out your pocket square on a flat surface.
2. Just below the halfway point, fold the pocket square. Fold up and then back down to form a pleat.
3. Repeat step 2 to create another pleat. Continue until you reach the bottom corner of the pocket square.
4. Fold the top corner down behind the pleats.

5. Then, fold the pocket square in half to make a smaller triangle.

6. Fold down one side at a 45 degree angle.

7. Finally, tuck it carefully into your pocket and neaten up if necessary.

Below is a diagrammatic explanation of the Monarch Fold:

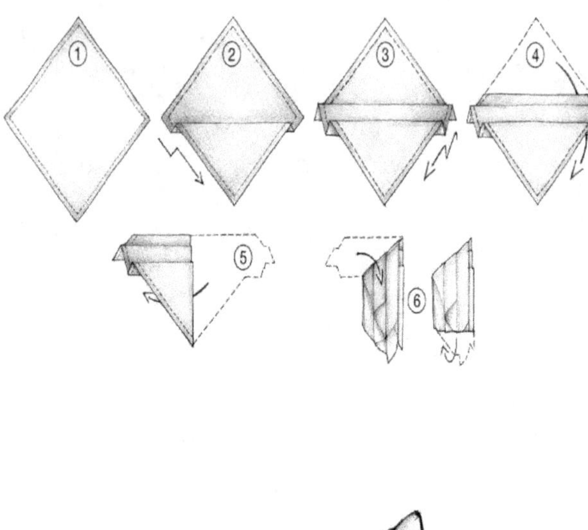

The Monarch fold

16. The Summit fold

This dynamic fold is perfect for that important board meeting. It's sleek and sharp and looks best with a conservative, business-like print or subtle solid color. Any fabric will do, but a stiffer one works best. The steps involved includes:

1. Lay a pocket square out and smooth it.
2. Fold in half diagonally, allowing the corners to overlap.
3. Fold the right corner over slightly.
4. Fold the bottom edge up to form another peak.
5. Fold the left corner down and to the right.

6. Tuck the bottom corner up around the back. Fold the right corner back.

7. Slide the fold into your pocket and close the deal!

Below is a diagrammatic explanation of the Summit Fold:

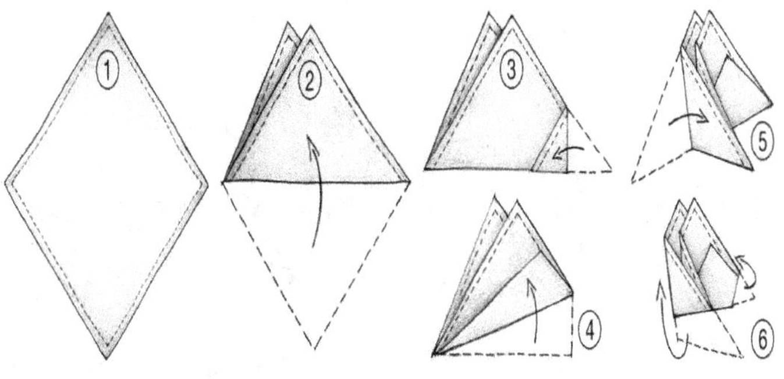

The Summit fold

17. The Rabbit fold

This fun and whimsical fold will add a dash of magic to your casual or formal ensemble. It looks amazing in both solid and printed pocket squares. The steps involved includes:

1. Smooth a pocket square down on a flat surface.
2. Fold it in half to form a triangle.
3. Fold all the corners up.
4. Fold the front corner down.
5. Then, fold one side over.
6. Fold the other side over.
7. Finally, place the folded fabric into your jacket pocket and perk the 'rabbit' ears up.

Below is a diagrammatic explanation of the Rabbit Fold:

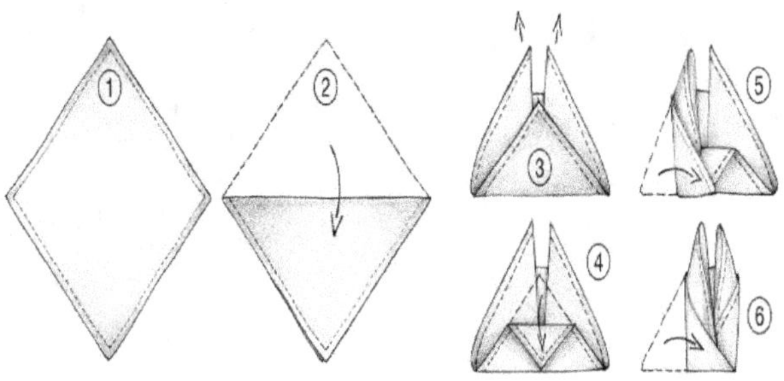

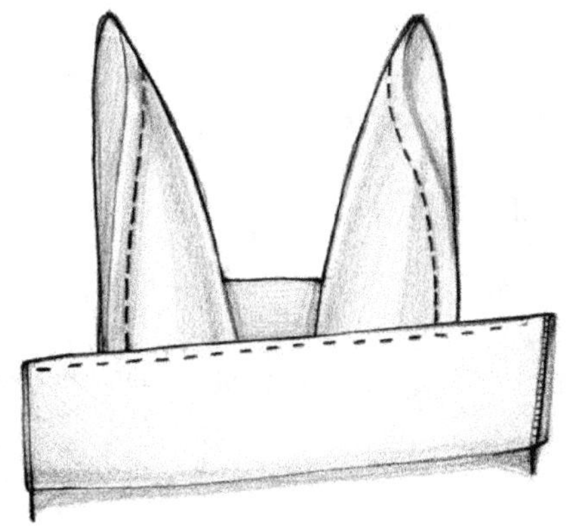

The Rabbit fold

18. The 3 Point Crown fold

This fold is timeless and sophisticated. It works best with solid colored pocket squares and looks amazing when paired with a double-breasted jacket. The steps involved includes:

1. Smooth the pocket square onto a flat surface.
2. Fold diagonally to create a triangle.
3. Fold up one of the bottom corners.
4. Do the same with the other one.
5. Fold in the side corner.
6. Fold in the other side corner.
7. Fold up the bottom to create the base.

8. Insert gently into your jacket pocket.

Below is a diagrammatic explanation of the 3 Point Crown Fold:

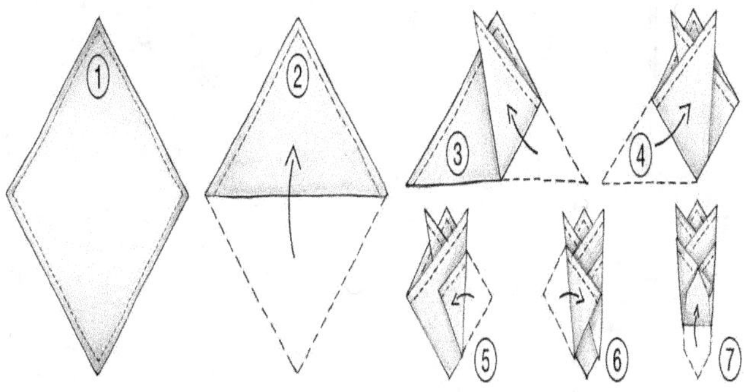

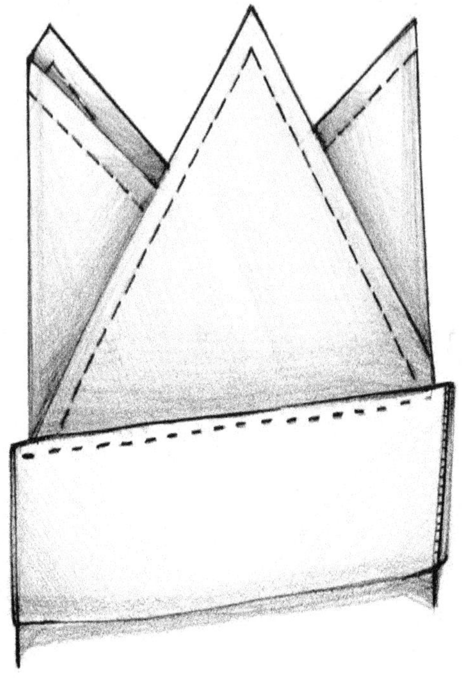

The 3 Point Crown fold

19. The 4 Angled Peaks fold

Scale a mountain of style with this neat fold. Features four angled peaks that draw the eye. Use a solid color square or one with a subtle print for best results.the steps involved includes:

1. Lay your square out flat.
2. Fold it in half diagonally to create a triangle.
3. Fold the bottom corner up to the top corner, ensuring they overlap.
4. Fold the new bottom corner up to the top, overlapping the existing points.
5. Fold the left corner under to form the base.

6. Slide the folded square into your pocket for a sharp look.

Below is a diagrammatic explanation of the 4 angled Peaks Fold:

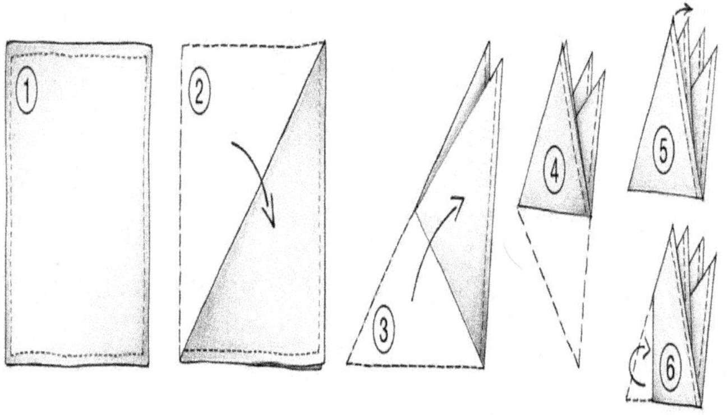

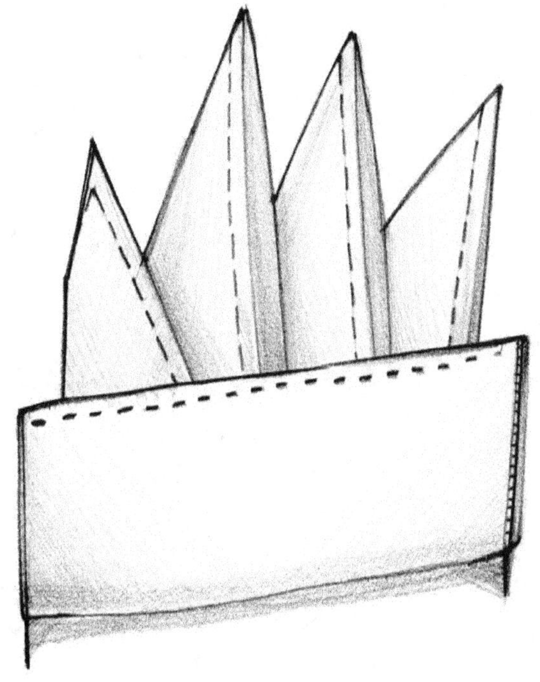

The 4 angled Peaks fold

20. The Switchback fold

This elegant fold is perfect for weddings and more formal occasions. It looks great in any fabric, whether it's a solid color or a bold print. Contrasting edges look especially good for this fold. The steps involved includes:

1. Lay your square out in a diamond-shaped orientation.
2. Fold it in half diagonally to make a triangle.
3. Fold the triangle in half to create a smaller one.
4. With the long side of the triangle facing you, fold back the right corner of the upper fabric.

5. Fold back the lower fabric of the right corner slightly so as not to cover the upper fabric fold.

6. Fold the entire left side back, tucking the corners behind.

7. Slip into your jacket pocket. Center and straighten as needed.

Below is a diagrammatic explanation of the 3 Point Crown Fold:

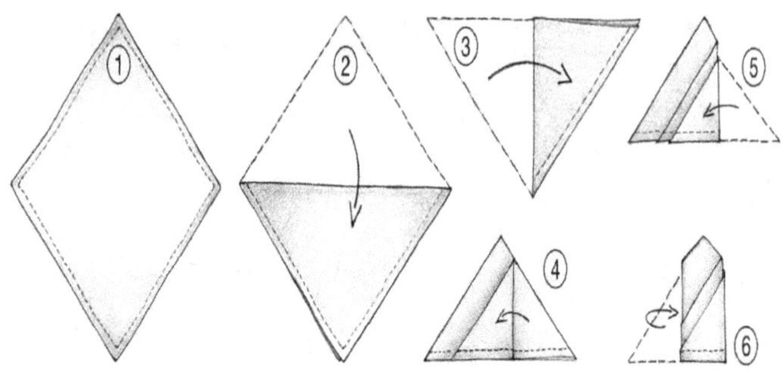

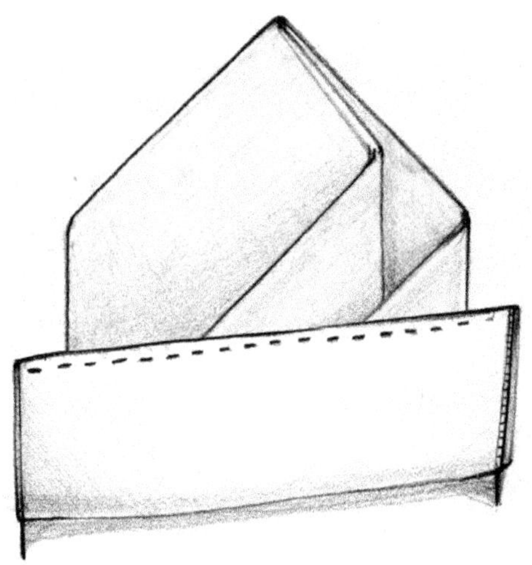

The Switchback fold

21. The Fancy Diamond Fold

Like a diamond, but so much better. This fold cleverly creates a look of facets. As you might imagine, this look is perfect for more formal occasions. Use a solid jewel tone square. The steps involved includes:

1. Flatten your fabric and smooth out.
2. Fold in half diagonally to make a large triangle.
3. Fold the right corner up to the opposite side.
4. Repeat step 3 with the left corner.
5. Fold the sides back.
6. Fold the bottom point up and under.
7. Slide into your pocket and adjust accordingly.

Below is a diagrammatic explanation of the
3 Point Crown Fold:

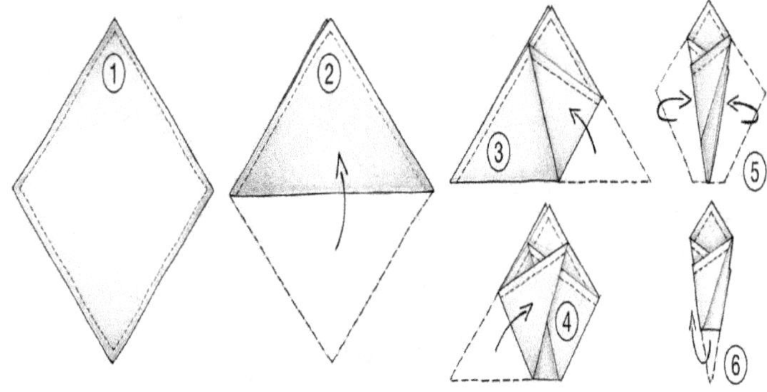

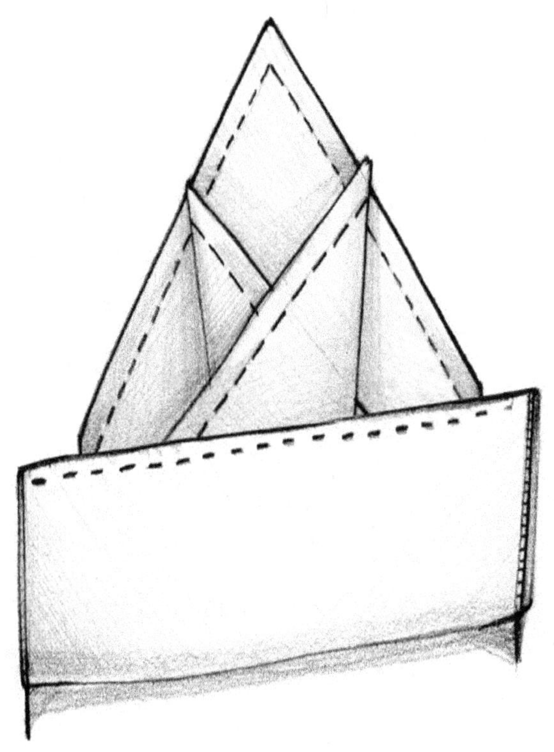

The Fancy Diamond Fold

22. The Wedge Fold

This relatively new fold is sleek and simple. It is great when worn with jeans and a casual blazer or even a more formal ensemble. The steps involved includes:

1. Lay your pocket square out on a flat surface.
2. Fold it in half to form a rectangle.
3. Fold the left side over to the right to create two overlapping squares.
4. Turn the pocket square so that both tips are facing up. Fold in the left side.
5. Now, fold in the right side.
6. Fold up the bottom and flip the pocket square over.
7. Tuck it into your breast pocket.

Below is a diagrammatic explanation of the Wedge Fold:

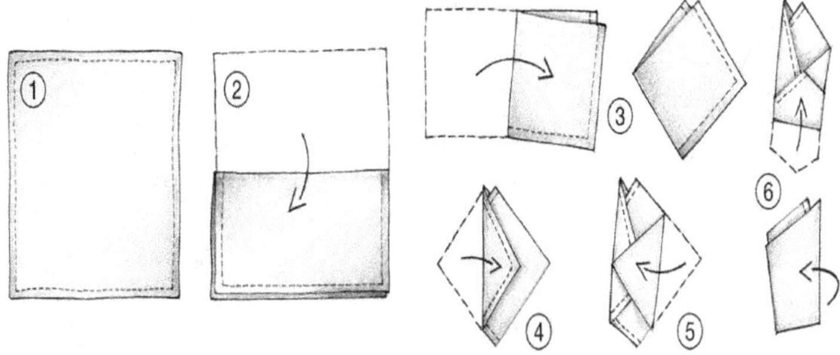

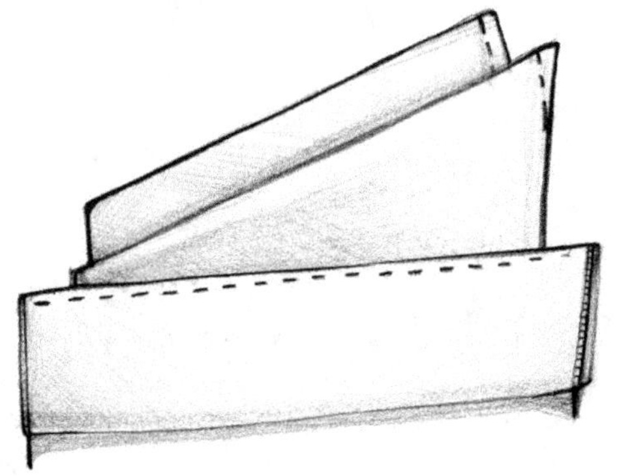

The Wedge Fold

23. The Tri-Fold Pocket Square Fold

Simple, Easygoing, Elegant. Just like you. This fold is the height of sophistication with its minimalist clean lines. Use a rigid fabric in a conservative pattern or solid color. Great look for the businessman. The steps involved includes:

1. Smooth out a pocket square on a flat surface.
2. Fold the top corner down to form a triangle.
3. Fold the triangle in half to make a smaller one.
4. With the long edge of the triangle facing you, fold the left corner up and over.
5. Do the same with the right corner.

6. Slip it in your pocket and primp as necessary.

Below is a diagrammatic explanation of the Trifold Fold:

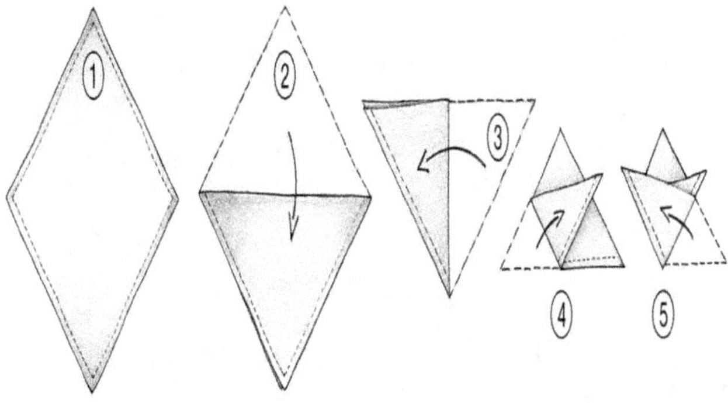

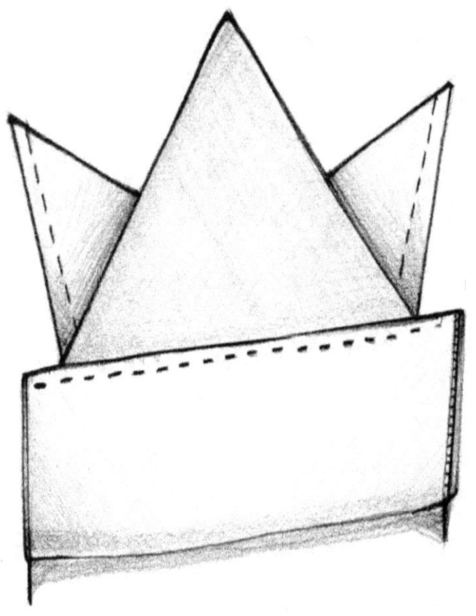

The Tri-Fold Pocket Square Fold

24. The Christmas Tree Pocket Square Fold.

Whether it's the most wonderful time of the year or you just so happen to be an arboreal fanatic, this fold is as charming as it gets. It looks best with a solid color pocket square, and silk makes the perfect fabric selection. The steps involved includes:

1. Lay the pocket square flat on a smooth surface.
2. Fold it in half diagonally to create a rectangle.
3. Fold it over again to make a square.
4. Take the corner with the open tips and begin to fold each leaf up.
5. Flip the pocket square over.

6. Next, fold one corner up.

7. Repeat the previous step on the opposite side.

8. Rotate the pocket square by 180 degrees.

9. Fold back each of the leaves, starting from the top and working your way down.

10. Tuck your tiny tree into your jacket pocket and charm the socks off of everyone you encounter.

Below is a diagrammatic explanation of the Christmas tree Fold:

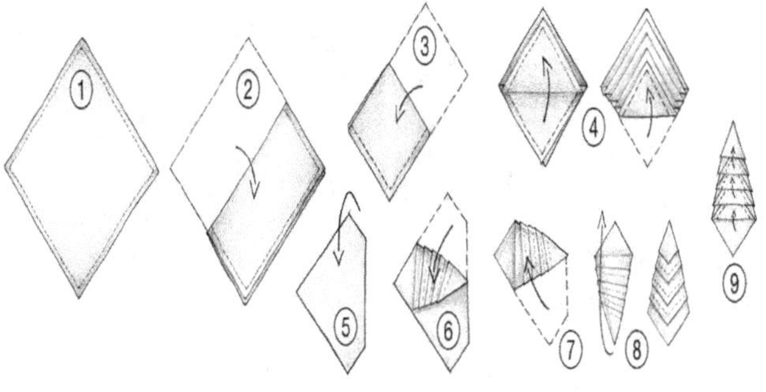

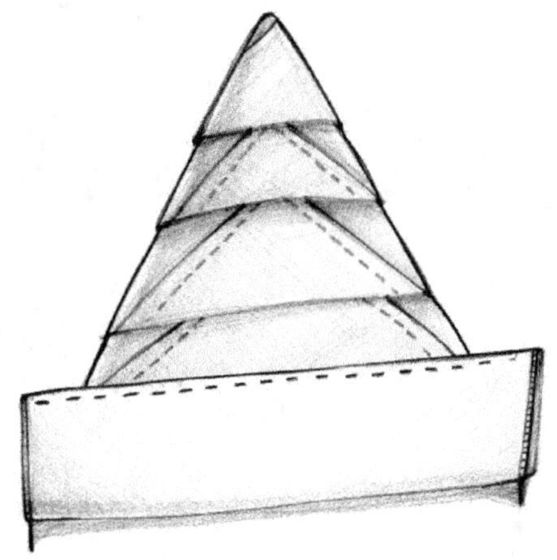

The Christmas Tree Pocket Square Fold.

Chapter 3

Summary

Now that our investigation into the creative realm of pocket squares has come to an end, let's take a moment to consider the twelve folds that can elevate an ensemble above the ordinary. This exploration of the nuances of folding techniques has been about accepting the refinement that comes with thoughtful clothing in addition to beauty.

Summary of the Twenty-four Folds

Each of the folds has a distinct melody that adds to a harmonious blend of style that exudes refinement and flare. With the timeless lines of the 3 Peaks Fold and the easygoing charm of the Monarch Fold, these methods offer a wide range of options for every situation. Knowing the subtleties of each fold gives you the ability to design a look that captures both the essence of the occasion and your own style.

Stressing How Adaptable Pocket Squares Are

Pocket squares are a testament to adaptability even when they are not folded. They move from dressy to casual with ease, moulding themselves to the shape of your outfit. A carefully folded silk square adds a regal grandeur to the lapel of a tuxedo. On the other hand, a linen pocket square gives a weekend ensemble a hint of carefree sophistication when it's tucked inside a blazer. The pocket square demonstrates that it is more than simply an accessory; rather, it is a revolutionary force in menswear thanks to its chameleon-like qualities.

This guide has been a thorough exploration of the world of sophisticated dressing, covering everything from selecting the ideal fabric to learning the fine art of sizing and placement to comprehending the historical tapestry that runs through pocket squares. A visual story that communicates more than words could ever hope to accomplish is made possible by the straight edges, flawless points, and imaginative folds.

A quote that inspires: "Elegance is an attitude."

In the world of fashion, elegance is an attitude that comes from within as much as a piece of clothes. True elegance is apparent as we work our way through the folds and textures of pocket squares; it is not limited by the material. It is our demeanour, our focus on the little things, and our assurance that speak for themselves. This attitude is reflected in the pocket square, a modest but significant item.

The inspirational saying, "Elegance is an attitude," acts as a compass. It serves as a reminder that our sense of style expresses who we are, no matter the setting or the outfit we select. As the classic piece of clothing, the pocket square is a fantastic representation of both refinement and the attitude that goes along with it.

ISBN 9798874184339
9 798874 184339
90000

4 FICTIONAL STORIES

Juicy Stories to pass time, love, adventure and deceptions.

ANGEL VIERA